SHORT BLACKS are gems of recent
Australian writing – brisk reads that quicken
the pulse and stimulate the mind.

SHORT BLACKS

THE BRAVE ONES

EAST TIMOR, 1999

JOHN BIRMINGHAM

SHORT ● BLACKS

Published by Black Inc.,
an imprint of Schwartz Publishing Pty Ltd
37–39 Langridge Street
Collingwood VIC 3066 Australia
enquiries@blackincbooks.com
www.blackincbooks.com

First published in Quarterly Essay 2, *Appeasing Jakarta: Australia's
complicity in the East Timor tragedy*, Black Inc., 2001.
This edition published 2015.

National Library of Australia Cataloguing-in-Publication entry:
Birmingham, John, 1964– author.
The brave ones : East Timor, 1999 / John Birmingham.
9781863957670 (paperback) 9781925203516 (ebook)
Short blacks ; no.5.
Political atrocities–Timor-Leste. Australia–Foreign relations–
Indonesia. Indonesia–Foreign relations–Australia. Timor-Leste–
History. Indonesia–History.
327.940598

Cover and text design by Peter Long.

JOHN BIRMINGHAM is the author of
He Died with a Felafel in His Hand,
*Leviathan: The Unauthorised Biography of
Sydney*, three popular fiction series and
two Quarterly Essays.

THE DOGS OF LOS PALOS

The Battalion's nickname was strictly and bitterly ironic. 'The Brave Ones'. A fighting unit with a proud history of child murder, rape, plunder and riot. You could tell when Battalion 745 had passed through because of their signature legacy of shallow graves, burnt buildings and drinking wells crammed with the mutilated remains of the dead peasants they were pledged to protect. In September 1999, they were quartered at the eastern end of Timor, at a barracks complex just north of Los Palos, a forlorn sort of place which had never really recovered from the fighting of 1975.

The town, a market centre, sat on a wide plain, a plateau really, the remnant of a huge primordial lagoon which had been pushed up out of the sea with the rest of the island millions of years ago. The ground rose slowly to hills in the south and lay within the confluence of two climatic systems, arid and baking to the north, wetter and somewhat milder to the south. Primal forest survived in these parts, around the base of the mountains where *Falintil*, the armed wing of resistance to Indonesian rule, had retreated before the advancing invaders in '76. Mostly, though, the land was given over to grazing and rice paddies, one of the few areas of Timor not dominated by the soaring, broken-backed cordillera running down its spine. Within Los Palos, low-rise, prefabricated steel buildings threw back the sun's glare as fiercely as the whitewashed limestone walls of the surviving Portuguese architecture, the best of which could be found in a Catholic college about five kilometres north of the town centre. Los Palos had been abandoned by its inhabitants during the invasion, most of them fleeing to the apparent safety of the nearby mountains, and the Indonesians, taking affront, had sacked the town.

Still, as one traveller wrote later, it wasn't so much that Los Palos had been savaged in the war. More that it had been depersonalised, like a settlement at the edge of a volcano's footprint, where the 'habit of living for the moment is engrained'. The people lived here, thought the writer Norman Lewis, not by choice but by an accident of fate, among temporary structures of corrugated iron, and they somehow kept going with a minimum of security and hope. The area had always been a centre of resistance to the invasion. A lot of young boys from Java, Madura and Bali had died around here, and the Indonesian armed forces had taken more than a generous measure of revenge on their behalf.

When Lewis journeyed through the district shortly after the travel ban on East Timor was lifted, he found an empty land known locally as the 'dead earth', because those who had filled it were gone. Driving along the coast road, it was possible to see traces of disappeared villages, outlined by strange geometrical beds of wild flowers or phallus-shaped gourds which had grown up within the boundaries of their ruins. Human activity, wrote Lewis, had come to an end.

Battalion 745, the Brave Ones, were tasked by Jakarta with making sure things stayed quiet. They were a territorial outfit, a bunch of second-raters, with a good percentage of their numbers made up by local men. Their training, equipment and operational doctrine were all inferior to the main force units of *Kostrad*, the army's strategic reserve, and *Kopassus*, the fearsome and much-hated special forces. They were not quite as bad as the militia, the military equivalent of those scabrous, stringy-legged wild dogs that haunt the streets of so many towns throughout the archipelago. But 745 were not what you'd call a disciplined or even a remotely formidable military force. Unless you happened to be an unarmed Timorese *paean*. In that case, as Ambrosio Alves discovered on Thursday, 9 September, an encounter with the Brave Ones could be just about the worst thing in the world.

The ninth was a busy day. Nearly a fortnight had passed since the referendum on East Timor's independence, and Jakarta's vengeance, the razing of the new nation, was well advanced. World attention, so distracted in 1975, had hardened against the Habibie government's mishandling of the ballot, but Jakarta seemed to be playing it out, buying as much time as the TNI (the Indonesian Armed Forces) and its militia surrogates needed to finish their work. On that particular day, Indonesian Foreign Minister Ali Alatas called for 'more time' to allow Indonesia to restore order. APEC foreign ministers meeting in Auckland had just demanded that Indonesia stop the killing, but Alatas and his ambassador in Canberra complained that a 48-hour deadline 'was unreasonable'. A fair-enough assessment, given that the 23 000 heavily armed troops and paramilitary police on duty in the province had so far proved themselves entirely incapable of stemming the violence. On the same day, the Australian government, facing a karmic payback on two and a half decades of weasel words and collaboration, announced it was doubling the size of its contribution to any peacekeeping force. The Governor of the 27th Province, Abilio Soares, who had deployed all the resources of state at his command in the effort to secure a vote against independence, said that Indonesia might not ratify the result anyway. TNI chief, General Wiranto, insisted that East Timor had become calmer after martial law, a claim dismissed by the Secretary General of the United Nations and met with weary contempt by the rest of world. The United Kingdom and New Zealand demonstrated their faith in the General's word by dispatching warships to the island; the United States Congress prepared a bill cutting off military aid as UNAMET's (United Nations Assistance Mission East Timor) compound in Dili came under heavy machine-gun fire. The few remaining staff were refusing to leave, saying they feared that one and a half thousand East Timorese who had taken shelter within their walls would be butchered as soon they left. As New York delayed their departure, José Ramos-Horta said the United Nations would be leaving them to almost certain death.

The world's attention had pulled in tight on that compound. That was partly a practical matter. There was little else it could see. The UN's regional staff and the hundreds of monitors from human rights groups such as Amnesty and the Carter Centre were going or gone, many of them hustled out of the province at gunpoint by the military. The position of hundreds of journalists, both Indonesian and international, who had covered the ballot and its aftermath, was increasingly untenable as they became the target of vicious harassment.

Matt Frei, from the BBC, described running towards the UN compound as a Timorese man nearby was 'hunted down like an animal'. A colleague of Frei's filmed the attack while hiding in a shack opposite the compound gates. 'It took only 30 seconds to hack the man to pieces,' said Frei. 'The attack was so ferocious that bits of him were literally flying off. The sound reminded me of a butchers' shop – the thud of cleaved meat, I'll never forget it.'

Keith Richburg, from the *Washington Post*, was struck by the resemblance of the Indonesian-sponsored militia to those he had seen in Africa during the Rwandan genocide. He took the blunt edge of a machete in the back from a militia-man while covering an attack near the UN headquarters that reminded him of similar close encounters in Mogadishu. It would all come back to him, he wrote, 'in my room at Dili's seaside Turismo Hotel, barricading the door against intruders, pulling the mattress to the floor to avoid stray bullets, positioning a tree branch near the bed to use as a last defence in case they made it through my flimsy fortification'. He'd left his bullet-proof vest in Nairobi, never believing he'd need it again, 'at least not in Indonesia, not for what was supposed to be an assignment covering economically booming Southeast Asia, in the last year of the century'.

There was one crucial difference, however. The danger in Africa had been random and spasmodic, a wrong place and wrong time deal. But Richburg and the other members of the press corps felt themselves specifically targeted by the military in East Timor, 'to close off the world's eyes and ears, so they could do their dirty work unimpeded'. In Mogadishu, he said, the media could cut a deal with the devil, hiring the militia to protect them as they went about their work. But the same primitive shakedown racket did not seem to operate in Dili. After the machete attack, Richburg and a few colleagues did pay local police, the *Brimob*, to guard the Turismo Hotel where they had holed up. The journalists even ponied up for the cops' meals and drink tab, putting it all on their hotel bill in the hope it might buy a little protection should a posse of goons from the *Aitarak* (or 'Thorn') militia decide to come over the walls. 'But by the third day,' he said, 'one of our protectors confided a secret to *Washington Post* special correspondent Atika Shubert, who speaks Indonesian: If the militia came, he told her late one night, he wouldn't shoot them to save us. He agreed with them, he told her: "They are doing good things for the country."' Richburg decided it was time to leave Dili. The fact was, a good number of *Aitarak* members were really TNI territorials and *Kopassus*, moonlighting as half-crazed savages who'd run amok after the vote. Various observer groups compiled dozens of statements from East Timorese who recognised members of the Indonesian military in the natty black tee-shirts of Eurico Guterres' nominally private army. The destruction of Dili was so thoroughly well organised and the intimidation and occasionally violent harassment of the observers so finely calibrated that the Indonesian government's obdurate, po-faced denials of state involvement were almost magnificent in their perversity. By the ninth of September however, they had achieved their aim. What the world knew of the crisis in East Timor was confined to a few hundred square metres of downtown Dili, comprising the UNAMET compound and the stories of those trapped inside. Conversely, of course, there was a blowback effect for the TNI. The shadowplay of the militia's vengeance, with the military as puppet master, had drawn the world's attention. Indonesia was getting its fifteen minutes of fame, but for all the wrong reasons. The tactics that had worked so well in earlier conflicts and covert operations, such as the original invasion of the Portuguese colony or the annexation of West Irian, proved less fruitful this time. In '75, Western governments connived at the ruse for geopolitical advantage. Non-aligned Indonesia was valued as an anti-communist foil and allowed or even encouraged in its misadventures. By 1999, a decade after the fall of the Berlin Wall and right after the implosion of the Asian economic miracle, the situation had changed.

The army officers behind the violence miscalculated the effect of their campaign. By forcing the last westerners and such a sorry collection of terrified refugees into the confines of the UN headquarters, they set up a story that the international press, and in particular the American media, was bound to exploit. The fact that the few journalists who remained to report the story got to play both participant and observer, so that they could represent themselves as crucial players in an unfolding tragedy, speaks of a certain lack of forethought on the part of those planning the destruction of East Timor. Indeed, the inability of the Indonesian elite to comprehend the tectonic shifts in both their own polity and the wider world was of critical importance to what happened in 1999, just as it was to the fall of Suharto and as it will be in the next ten years, when their republic either recovers or disintegrates. As Paul Keating stated, around this time Indonesia stopped being a country in US eyes and became an issue. The madness of September '99 simply reinforced Indonesia's new status, as if the violence was an allegory for the disintegration of the whole country.

On the ninth, however, all that mattered was the compound. Throughout the night, the air above was constantly rent by automatic gunfire, with tracers zipping past into the hills behind, making escape impossible. Thousands of people sheltered in a school next door, all fearing an attack which came with militia charging the campus, while TNI troops and *Brimob*, the paramilitary police, fired on the compound. The panic induced was so great that many parents simply threw their children onto and over the barbed wire which sat atop the wall guarding the UN buildings, hoping to get them away from the marauders. A 26-year-old woman described the assault for Amnesty International after she had been evacuated to Darwin:

> They came in with swords which they were swinging at people, but they did not hit anyone ... The people inside the compound were panicking and some were so scared that they jumped over the fence which had barbed wire on top. Some parents were so terrified for the safety of their children

that they just hurled their babies and young
children over the fence. Many of them were
cut on the wire or hurt when they fell on
the other side. I could see that the army
were playing a very direct role in this attack.
They were shooting in the air trying to
frighten and panic the people and looting all
our possessions.

Vision of the attack was beamed out on
satellite links, a squalling, claustrophobic
catherine-wheel of images. Screaming women
and children, wild-eyed men, UN staff and even
other journalists – yelling, gesturing wildly for
blankets or cardboard or coats, for anything
to lay over the wire, all of them flinching and
ducking instinctively at the roar of automatic
weaponry outside. Only rumours, terrible and
perhaps archetypal, relayed any sense of what
was happening beyond the immediate range of
the cameras. The *Guardian*'s John Aglionby said

he'd been told by villagers of men being marched
to the waterfront then gunned down and bayo-
neted, an echo of atrocities from the invasion in
'75. Others spoke of bodies, headless and limb-
less, stacked to the rafters of police stations.
Perhaps it was true, but probably not.

The urgency of those horror stories, the way
they sparked and jumped so easily from the lips
of a terrified refugee and onto the front pages
of metro dailies all over the globe, testified to
the moral bankruptcy of the Indonesian regime.
Their credit was gone, and it says a lot about the
attachment psychosis of the New Order regime
that it still couldn't help but play out the game.
The essence of politics is conflict, but in stable
societies this is ritualised and channelled into
non-destructive forms. There are limits to action.
The New Order, however, which came to power
via the enormously bloodthirsty coup and counter
coup of 1965–6, seems never to have internalised
this lesson, that political development proceeds

from anarchy to order – not just to organised terror. At the heart of its extreme reaction to any form of challenge there must have been a corrosive doubt in its own legitimacy. For a regime apparently so certain of its command prerogative, it invested hugely in repressing the merest hints of defiance throughout the archipelago. Freedom was evil, dissent was subversion and its own citizens could not be trusted. That deeply ingrained pattern of political psychosis was allowed a full flowering in East Timor – and so, while the siege of the UN compound in Dili served variously as metaphor and melodrama, and as a channel for the world's frustrated rage, in the dark beyond CNN's failing, constricted field of vision the blood-dimmed tide was loosed. The Catholic Church announced that six nuns in Baucau and a priest in Suai had been slain by militia. The first intimations of a genocidal evil began to seep out of West Timor. And Ambrosio Alves encountered the Brave Ones.

Little is known of Ambrosio's last hours. He was grabbed up in the village of Asalaino by soldiers from Battalion 745 and members of the Team Alpha militia. He was beaten to death and found two months later, in a shallow grave with another, unknown victim. The significance of his passing lies in the fact that he is the first known victim of 745's withdrawal from the province. We know a lot about the passage of the Brave Ones through East Timor because one of their last victims was Sander Thoenes, a Dutch journalist. He had the bad luck to strike a couple of battalion outriders, either territorial or Team Alpha, the same crew who bailed up British reporter John Swain on the second day of INTERFET's (International Force East Timor) lodgement. Swain had hired a taxi with an American photographer Chip Hires and was crawling through the hills outside Dili when 745's convoy enveloped them. Motorcycle riders began hammering at the vehicle, pulling on the handles. One of them turned his rifle on the driver Sanjo Ramos, smashing him in the head with such force that he lost an eye. Swain later said that as Battalion commander Major Yacob Sarosa pulled up, he yelled at the journalists. 'These people are East Timorese too. They are very angry, very angry with [the] UN and you Westerners. You must understand.' The Brave Ones then 'arrested' Swain's interpreter, Anacleto Bendito da Silva, forcing him into a truck at gunpoint. The westerners never saw him again, but a Battalion sergeant, Hermenegildo dos Santos, a *Falintil* informer who later returned to East Timor, revealed that he had been murdered during the battalion's stopover in Dili.

The Brave Ones were really taking care of business that night. An hour later they're thought to have ambushed Thoenes, the Jakarta correspondent for the *Financial Times*. A local motorcycle chauffeur testified that he gave the Dutchman a lift to the suburb of Becora, where three uniformed soldiers opened up on them with automatic weapons. A single round took Thoenes in the back, ripping through his heart and lungs, causing death within minutes. He was mutilated post-mortem. A nearby TNI post did not intervene in the shooting, or offer the journalist medical aid, nor bother to contact INTERFET.

Between the murders of Thoenes and Ambrosio Alves back in Los Palos, the Brave Ones racked up nearly two dozen civilian kills, some bodies left burning in ditches by the side of dirt roads, some dumped in rice paddies, others in shallow graves or simply in fields where they had been shot in the back while trying to flee. Quite a few dropped down village wells – a disposal technique with a bonus pay-off, the poisoning of scarce water supplies during the island's severe dry season. They made a mistake killing Thoenes, though. One of his freelance employers, the *Christian Science Monitor*, was so appalled that they dispatched another reporter, Cameron Barr, to chase down the story of Battalion 745, which seemed to have marked its route out of East Timor with a trail of corpses and ruin. As he traced their withdrawal, along the coast road and through the dead earth, Barr heard that the Brave Ones had wiped out six people as they swept through the town of Baucau. A young man in Fuiloro, near Los Palos, explained how 745 had snatched up and murdered his brother. Investigators confirmed they were sure the battalion was responsible for Thoenes' death. And in Los Palos he found Sergeant dos Santos, who gave Australian police officers detailed information about his former outfit's war crimes. Barr's reconstruction of the Brave Ones' last days shot holes in the TNI cover story that the unholy disorganised bloodswarm which blew through the eastern half of the island was chaotic, objectless and unplanned. It was, as everyone could see – and as many had warned for months before the referendum – a state-sponsored program, part vengeance and deterrence, but also encompassing barbarism for its own sake. The only question was, which state? The formally recognised government of Indonesia, headed by President Habibie and represented abroad by Ali Alatas? Or another state? A ghost nation existing within the formal structures of the republic, a revenant of Suharto's New Order regime. For that vast, conflicted network of military and corporate combines, well-connected robber barons, state apparatchiks and First Family business concerns did not pass away with the untimely departure of their Emperor. As former Indonesian minister Lakesmana Sukardi put it, 'The pathologies of the previous regime remain in the system.'

This should not come as a surprise. The stripping of formal state power from Suharto and the *Golkar* party was a sea change in the affairs of Indonesia. Given the harsh treatment doled out to opponents as a matter of course during the

Suharto era, the eruption of democracy protests in the late 1990s was a testimony to the strength of the pressures building beneath the surface of the republic's polity. But while the removal of the New Order's supreme leader did clear a path into the open for a myriad of challengers, the machinery that maintained him in the presidential palace was not so easily swept aside. Exceedingly powerful economic and political interests were exposed and threatened by the lurch towards democracy. For the New Order was not simply a coercive dictatorship. It also co-opted potential competitors, such as military officers or religious and political leaders, rewarding their allegiance with lucrative positions in the corporate state. Individual beneficiaries of that system might find themselves persecuted as the monolith began to crumble, but the system itself – massive, tenacious and inherently corrupt – was more durable. Speaking in Sydney earlier this year at a seminar organised by the

Australia–Asia Institute, the Australian-based
Indonesian academic Dr. George J. Aditjon-
dro described the current Indonesian political
system as New Order Mark 2, and asked what
sort of democratic revolution it was that left the
corrupt apparatus of a regime in place. It was
this surviving structure which stood behind the
carnage in East Timor, mostly because the Indonesian army, which formed one of three pillars
of the New Order was, as Bob Lowry put it, still
trapped by the formulas of the past. The ham-
fisted thuggery of their surrogates' campaign
for autonomy, and the savagery of their reaction to defeat, should have come as no surprise.
The entire history of the province was leading
towards such an eruption, and the brutality of
outfits like the Brave Ones was less a matter of
uncontrolled rage than finely nuanced policy.

Amnesty International, which devoted
extensive resources to covering the pre- and
post-ballot period in East Timor, described a

'well-organised plan to remove local residents from one area even before the ballot result was announced'. The smooth meshing of militia and Indonesian government forces gave the lie to Jakarta's denials of any such formal liaison. The day after the vote, in the Aileu District, Police Mobile Brigade personnel drove into four villages 'and began firing into the air'. Amnesty's report continues:

> Militiamen then arrived, ordering people to leave and burning houses down. They gathered people together and forced the people to state whether or not they had voted for independence. Those who had were told that they would have to stay in East Timor and that they would 'die'. In the town of Aileu itself, an observer reported that local TNI officials ordered people to leave their homes, register their names and state which way they had voted in the ballot. They were

then told to gather their belongings and move towards the police headquarters in Aileu. According to the observer, one group of people claimed they had been told they would be going to the towns of Atambua or Kupang in West Timor; if they refused to go they would be considered to have voted for independence and would die.

It is inconceivable, given the magnitude and the logistic demands of the scorched earth operation in East Timor, that army chief General Wiranto was unaware of its existence. The broad outline of the strategy was exposed time and again by foreign journalists and aid workers with direct access to the territory in the months before the ballot.

Operation *Wiradharma*, as it was known to senior *Kopassus* officers, 'would have required at least his [Wiranto's] condonement', according to the United Nation's special investigator, former Australian diplomat James Dunn. Dunn's investigations found that the spasm of 'so-called militia violence' that culminated in massive deportations and destruction in September '99 was not a spontaneous outburst by those who favoured integration, but rather the outcome of a plan by TNI generals, executed for the most part by officers of elite *Kopassus* units. His report found that the Indonesian military sponsored the establishment of the militia, providing training, arms, money and even drugs on occasion.

While Dunn has often been maligned by Suharto apologists as a die-hard member of Australia's East Timor lobby – a charge which did nothing to stop the UN appointing him to such a sensitive position – his report to the UN merely restated the conclusions of Indonesia's own National Human Rights Commission. The Commission reported in January 2000 that there were strong links between the TNI, various arms of the Indonesian police (POLRI and *Brimob*), the provincial government and the militias. The violence was 'the result of a systematic campaign' based on 'extensive planning'. The militias were 'under the direct co-ordination of the TNI', not just one or two rogue, lowly placed officers. Their mobilisation 'was in line with various policies of the military leadership' and 'was accomplished through political terror. Murder, kidnappings and forced displacement were committed by members of the TNI, POLRI, government bureaucracy and the militias':

> After the popular consultation, violence increased drastically throughout East Timor, including murders, kidnappings, rape, property destruction, theft of homes and property, the burning and destruction of military installations, offices and civilian residences, with the goal of forced deportation. Members of the TNI, POLRI and the militias were the key figures responsible for

this campaign which involved the creation of conditions, choice of acts committed, scheduling and planning of the forced deportation. This campaign was initiated to convince the international community that the results of the popular consultation should be doubted and that the people of East Timor would rather choose to live safely in West Timor...

Of course, that was a choice denied the two dozen unlucky souls who chanced across Battalion 745 on their own journey to the west. The day after Ambrosio Alves fetched up in a hole, two brothers, Florentino and Florencio Branco, were strongarmed out of their village, Home Baru. Their bodies are believed to have been dropped into a well inside the Battalion compound to rest with a few of their neighbours. When Cameron Barr pulled through on the trail of his colleague's killers, he found the well surrounded by tall cornstalks and partially covered over with rusted corrugated iron. It was possible, with the sun in just the right position, to make out the tangle of rotting limbs and torsos at the bottom.

Three days later, another two members of the extended Branco clan joined Florentino and Florencio. On the night of the 12th, Martinho Branco had fled into the rice paddies with his family and their friends, the Belos. 745 tracked them down and fired over their heads, threatening to kill everyone if they made the troops wade through the paddy sludge to lay hands on them. Barr writes:

> The families reluctantly stood up and
> walked toward the waiting soldiers. Belo
> and Branco were immediately arrested.
> Without explanation the 745 soldiers also
> grabbed each man's eldest child, two teenage
> boys uninvolved in politics. Juliao de Assis
> Belo's wife, Filomena de Jesus Freitas, was
> devastated to see her son in the hands of the

soldiers. 'If you want to kill someone, take me, not him,' she pleaded. They ignored her and marched the men and boys along a dirt road that divides two large rice fields. Ms. Freitas and Branco's wife, Maria do Ceu, watched their husbands and sons walk out of sight. Gunshots were heard a few minutes later. The women prayed.

At mid-afternoon Freitas found the courage to go to the Battalion 745 compound to ask after the men and boys. She was told that they had not been arrested. The next day the people in the neighbourhood began to search. At dawn on Sept. 15, they found Belo, Branco, and Branco's son Marcelio in an area about five minutes' walk from where the families had hidden in the fields. The corpses were partially burned, but Freitas recognised her husband's face and trousers. Her son, Elder, was nearby, at the bottom of a well.

The Battalion was occupied for the next few days breaking down their HQ and transporting the bulk of their personnel to Lautem, a small beach settlement by the Wetar Strait, from where they would be shipped back to Java. Those troops remaining in Los Palos ransacked their barracks and burned about three-quarters of the town, including the UN buildings, the market, and the power, water and communications facilities. Their work done, they saddled up a convoy consisting of dozens of army trucks, some stolen civilian vehicles and a few dozen motorcycles – the latter driven by Team Alpha members. Sergeant dos Santos told Barr that the convoy was not filled with overwrought men bent on revenge. The soldiers were happy to leave and indeed seemed delighted with their orders to carry out a scorched earth retreat. As Battalion CO Major Yacob Sarosa stood by, a lieutenant told dos Santos, 'If you find anything on the way, just shoot it.' According to the NCO, Sarosa had previously warned his men that if Jakarta's preferred option went down in the ballot, 'they would have to destroy everything.'

The 21st was the Brave Ones' last full day in East Timor and they held nothing back. It was also a day on which they brushed up close against their own destruction and all but touched off a war between Indonesia and Australia. Their first victims were Abreu and Egas da Costa, murdered just a few minutes after the convoy had left their own barracks ablaze at Laga. Their deaths were witnessed by Zelia Maria Barbosa Pinto, who hid in an irrigation ditch as she heard the convoy approaching. The da Costa brothers, doubling on a motorbike, weren't as lucky. Their own engine noise masked the approach of the trucks until it was too late and the battalion outriders were on top of them. Somebody in the convoy yelled out that they were terrorists, and as Abreu backed away from the motorcycle and screamed at his brother, 'We're going to die,' the soldiers opened up on them.

Someone shot Abreu's leg out from under him as he ran. He fell, staggered up and made it a few more feet before a round slapped into the back of his skull and pitched him into the paddy water. His brother didn't get that far; he was shot in the stomach before he could run more than ten feet. Zelia Pinto watched a soldier walk over and bayonet him.

The da Costas had been about a hundred yards from the turn-off to their home in the village of Buruma. But it's a moot point whether they'd have lived if they'd made their run just a few minutes earlier. 745 moved inexorably through Buruma and the sister village of Caibada that morning. Lucinda Da Silva took a shotgun blast in the chest. Elisita da Silva was machine-gunned while cowering behind a bush with her baby daughter, Cesarina. The toddler's grand-mother witnessed the shooting, which killed Elisita and shattered Cesarina's right thigh. A few miles down the road, a couple of soldiers straggling behind the convoy killed Victor Belo, who was returning to his home thinking the danger had passed. Carlos da Costa Ribeiro, a former teacher who had stayed hidden in his house, was hunted down and shot in the head.

Later in the day a couple of Timorese youths, who remain unidentified, were arrested, beaten and taken to Manatutu. They were never seen again. The village itself was annihilated, with 98 per cent of the buildings razed to the ground. When the UN came through a few days later, not a living soul could be found in Manatutu and the surrounding countryside appeared to have been emptied of life.

745 and Team Alpha drove through the old Portuguese quarter of Baucau, the second city of East Timor and a major staging point for TNI operations throughout the centre and eastern reaches of the island. From there they took the coast road west for Dili, where they bundled up the journalists Swain and Hires, before killing

their colleague Sander Thoenes. As the convoy moved along the main Becora road, with gutted, burned-out houses slipping by on both sides, soldiers in the back of the trucks whooped it up, firing into the air. A local who was caught out in the open, Manuel Andreas, was shot in the back as he tried to escape down a ruined side street. The convoy halted for a few hours at the TNI barracks in Dili, where they refuelled, ate dinner and murdered John Swain's interpreter. Before they drove out later that evening on the last leg of their retreat, a local military commander asked them to refrain from further bloodshed. Within half an hour they had driven into a potentially catastrophic showdown with the second cavalry regiment of the Australian Army.

*

The Australian modified light armoured vehicle, the ASLAV to its friends, is really not that light. Or friendly. It weighs in at about thirteen tons, depending on its configuration. 2 Cav, the Second Cavalry Regiment of the Australian Army, runs up to half a dozen variants based on three different hull types. The ASLAV 25, an eight-wheeled, three-man reconnaissance vehicle, carries an M242 25 mm Bushmaster cannon, a chain gun which can discretely place a single high-explosive incendiary cartridge into the heart of a problem, day or night, from up to 2000 metres away. Alternately, should you prove reluctant to come around to the Cav's way of thinking, the Bushmaster could hose you down at a rate of 200 rounds per minute. The ASLAV 25 can also mount two machine-guns in its turret, which is fully stabilised and equipped with a thermal imaging day/night gun sight. Its sister vehicle, the ASLAV PC, which is designed to carry seven troops into harm's way, comes with a 12.7 mm machine-gun and a day/night gun sight at the Crew Commander's station. Standing next to an ASLAV, your average machete-wielding villain is immediately dwarfed by its blunt mass and, more subtly, by the promise of mayhem contained within its brutish frame. As the Australian Army's Third Brigade secretly worked up a concept of operations for lodgement in East Timor (a week before President Habibie invited them in), 2 Cav's thirteen-ton armoured vehicles were among the first units chosen.

The ASLAV's offensive capabilities and the training and commitment of the men who drove them were the reasons why armed peacekeepers were never going to be welcome in East Timor in the pre-ballot period. General Cosgrove made it abundantly clear at the start of INTERFET's mission that trying to intimidate his soldiers would be a very different matter to lording it over unarmed civilians. With a neutral, heavily armed force in place, the TNI's scorched earth policy would have been prohibitively expensive, or even impossible to carry through in the face of opposition from the likes of the Second Cavalry Regiment. The antipathy and reserve of the Indonesian forces which prevailed in Dili when INTERFET arrived was partly an expression of that. The TNI had many more troops in place, but behind the comparatively small number of INTERFET personnel stood the threat of intervention by the armed forces of those states that had contributed them, including (though not limited to) Australia's traditional allies, the United States and Great Britain. The appearance of that foreign armour on Dili's ruined streets signalled to all sides in the East Timor conflict that things had changed; specifically, the immunity to armed sanction enjoyed by pro-Jakarta forces had ended. This transitional phase was the most dangerous moment of the crisis, the point at which miscalculation by INTERFET or foolhardiness by militia or TNI units could easily flash into a wider, international conflict. Into this situation rode the Brave Ones.

On the night of 21 September, the second day of INTERFET's mission, half a dozen ASLAVs, disbursed in two groups, were squatting astride the main east-west road through Dili. While the TNI's senior officer in East Timor, Major General Kiki Syahnakri, had proved entirely co-operative and had indeed rendered invaluable assistance to INTERFET during the taut period immediately before and after the arrival of Australian combat forces, Dili was still infested with hundreds of militia bandits and ill-disciplined Indonesian troops. At all hours of the day and night they tore through the devastated city in trucks and cars, screaming abuse and levelling their weapons at the Australians. Under the rules of engagement they could have been shot at any time for making such threatening gestures, but the Australian troops restrained themselves despite the heat and stress and physical demands of carrying full combat loads. That stress should not be underestimated. Foot patrols ran all day and night. Sleep was snatched in short bursts among rubble and burning refuse. Bob Breene, in one of the first serious military accounts of the INTERFET mission, described the environment as an assault on the senses. 'Smoke, stench and dust filled nostrils and stung eyes. Buildings were on fire or smouldering black shells.' Rubbish, dead dogs and human filth lay everywhere, piled up into mounds wherever large numbers of East Timorese had sheltered in the last hours, such as down at the port. Very few civilians remained in the town proper and nobody walked anywhere. Everyone ran. Nighttime was even weirder. 'Bizarre and dangerous', according to Breene, a city of the dead under a smoky red glow, with long convoys of trucks crammed with soldiers and loot rolling through the streets while spasmodic gunfire and explosions could still be heard in the distance.

The first Australians ashore, an advance group of about 1500 paratroopers, special forces, assault pioneers, cavalry and airborne infantry, worked in a hyper-stressed, uncertain atmosphere. Indonesia still had tens of thousands of armed men on the ground, and despite Syahnakri's genuine desire to avoid any conflict, everyone was aware that these were the same troops General Wiranto had supposedly had so much trouble controlling over the past month. Ramping up the tension, the Australians, most of them very young men, were at last close enough to reach out and touch the material consequence of the TNI's failure. Bodies rotted in drinking wells, drainage ditches and ruined buildings. Some, writes Breene, had been burned to destroy evidence, leaving behind nothing more than ashes and bone.

> Some bodies bore signs of torture and all had been mutilated. In some cases, hands and heads had been cut off in a crude and brutal attempt to hide the victim's identity. The body of a young woman, her hands

bound and throat cut, abandoned in a toilet
area awash with her blood, was a shocking
discovery for the diggers who found her.
For many young soldiers these were the first
bodies they had seen. Soldiers who had to
recover and place remains in body bags, or
re-bury bodies for health reasons, recalled
that they would never forget the smell and
how it lingered on their clothing long after
they had finished their gruesome duties.

In some buildings there were signs of
multiple murders, the dark brown of dried
blood accentuated by white tiled floors. At
several sites floors were covered in blood
and gore; bits and pieces of people. There
were thick sprays of blood and brain tissue
along walls at a height suggesting that
victims had been forced to kneel before
being shot through the head. Limbs,
chunks of flesh and entrails were scattered
about in other buildings amongst pools

of blood suggesting frenzied attacks with knives and machetes. The diggers followed blood trails of victims who had been hacked, and then fled, bleeding profusely before succumbing to further blows; dying before their bodies were dragged away. There were machetes and clubs covered in gore, abandoned after being used to butcher victims. Bloody drag marks suggested that scores of bodies had been dragged away for disposal.

In contrast to the 23 000 TNI and *Brimob* troops, who had been strangely ineffective in the face of this slaughter, INTERFET's comparatively small number of personnel began locking down the city immediately. The ASLAV roadblock was part of a campaign to quickly establish their dominance. The armoured carriers were parked in a herringbone arrangement at two sites to snare single truckloads of militia and others who still haunted the city in the first few days. The soldiers manning the road block had orders to stop anybody who was armed but not in uniform. They had no idea that Battalion 745 was coming through the night towards them.

Around ten o'clock in the evening, the Brave Ones' motorcycles, riding point on what had grown into a 60-truck convoy, ran up hard against the ASLAV checkpoint. After looting and killing their way across the island from Los Palos, 745 and their Team Alpha cohorts were emotionally unprepared for any resistance. They'd been ordered to chill out back at the Dili barracks, but as the convoy growled and squeaked to a halt in the dark, angry militiamen and soldiers began to shout and wave at the Australians, demanding they move aside. The Brave One's vanguard presented as a sort of B-movie vision of some pirate biker gang from Hell, a rat bastard outfit in black tee-shirts, camouflage pants, long hair and bandanas, with axes in their eyes and guns at the ready. The Australians – assault pioneers, a couple of rifle platoons and six pairs of snipers – were all kitted out with body armour and night vision equipment, giving them a distinctly threatening, insectile, other-worldly appearance beneath their kevlar helmets. Unbeknownst to the territorials and militia, who were blind in the dark, their every move was being observed in the cool green glow of low-light amplification systems.

The Australian ranking officers, a pair of lieu-tenants, one of whom spoke Bahasa, informed the motorcycle escort of his orders to detain anyone they came across armed and not in uniform. The riders revved their bikes as their spokesman blustered and demanded passage through the blockade. The voices grew loud and more agi-tated as it became obvious that 745 might not be allowed through immediately. As more Aus-tralian soldiers quietly deployed to support their leader, Indonesians and Timorese dropped from the backs of trucks, unshipping their weapons, crying out, demanding to know the cause of the delay. Some of the hard chargers of Team Alpha and 745 began to shoulder their rifles, unaware they could be seen in the dark.

Under the UN-sanctioned rules of engagement, they were now dead men. But the Australians, outnumbered many times over, did not open up on them. They did not respond in any obvious way. No orders were given, but each man slowly raised his Austeyr F 88 from the hip. Guns on the ASLAVS tracked around smoothly, settling on the trucks full of Indonesian soldiers. Photon streams poured out of laser designators, painting bright dots – visible only through the diggers' night vision goggles – on the foreheads and chests of those men fated to die first.

As INTERFET commander Major General Peter Cosgrove said later, it is no exaggeration to say that the future of Australia's relationship with Indonesia hung in the balance for the next few minutes. Besides 745's military personnel, those trucks also carried the family members of some departing soldiers. Mixed in with their heavily armed, undisciplined escorts, many would have died in a fire fight. So tenuous was the situation in Dili, and so poisonous was the relationship between the two countries at that moment, that everything then turned on the actions of the young lieutenants and the men standing behind them.

The Howard Government was well aware of the potential for such an incident to spin out of control and had warned the Australian electorate to prepare itself for heavy casualties. Instancing the sort of scenarios that could unfold, a Current Issues Brief prepared by the Parliamentary Library's Foreign Affairs, Defence and Trade Group on 21 September contemplated a range of outcomes in the territory, including high-level armed conflict between the Australian Defence Force (ADF) and the TNI.

If such a worst case scenario were to eventuate the consequences could initially include booby traps, land mines, snipers, maritime mines in or around the harbour, low-level skirmishes, ambush, mortars, and attacks launched from shoulder launched surface-to-air missiles. INTERFET could face terrorist attack, for example, a truck bomb driven into an INTERFET compound or hand grenades thrown into a town market. If the TNI directly confronted the ADF and the situation escalated, the ADF would probably seek close air support which would include attacks on the TNI from helicopter gunships. The TNI in turn could seek air support and Indonesian F-16s could confront ADF F-18s over the skies of the territory.

The paper went on to dismiss such a possibility as remote, mostly because the Indonesian armed forces were significantly outclassed by the ADF in such capabilities. But the spectre of disaster was ever present with heavily armed, keyed-up members of the two forces intertwined in such a volatile setting. It needed only one misfortune to escalate, such as the unanticipated 'capture' of Battalion 745 in the ASLAV's militia snare, and all of Cosgrove's and Syahnakri's efforts at a smooth handover would fall through. Escalation was avoided in this case only when the Australian command decided to allow the convoy through.

Cosgrove has used the example of this roadblock more than once to illustrate the importance of training, discipline and modern equipment. He saw it, quite rightly, as a small moment of vindication. But it was also a failure, a nexus point at which the full weight of twenty-four years of accumulated strategic folly, moral poverty, infamy, lies, naïveté and self-delusion suddenly dropped onto the shoulders of a handful of young soldiers.

It had long been an unspoken tenet of Australian strategic guidance that while this country probably would not lose a war with Indonesia, it certainly could not afford such a conflict. The relative capabilities of each nation's military forces actually favour Australia. But Australian policy makers have long understood that as a small, white outpost of the former British Empire, Australia's place among its neighbours cannot be taken for granted. Colonialism left a bitter taste in the mouths of many nationalist leaders in the region, and Australia's long commitment to the White Australia Policy still rankles – even though it is the most egregious form of hypocrisy for some regional states to claim the moral high ground on matters of racial tolerance.

In spite of excellent ties with powers such as Japan and Korea, Australian interests can still be damaged by the hostility of individual states. For instance, Malaysian Prime Minister Mahathir's implacable opposition to Australian initiatives such as APEC has seen our diplomats barred from a number of important regional forums and trading groups. In the 1990s, our close relationship with Indonesia, the first among equals in ASEAN, counterbalanced such antagonism. Australian commitment to regional institutions and operations such as the peace plan in Cambodia demonstrated a willingness to work with and for the region, and lent credence to Prime Minister Keating's oft-stated conviction that we should seek our security within Asia, not from Asia. For a few months in late 1999, that admirable objective was threatened by developments in East Timor. For a few minutes on the night of 21 September, it was in mortal peril. The gulf between Australia and Indonesia was already yawning when President Habibie bowed to world pressure to allow a peace-keeping force into the disputed territory. How much greater would the chasm now be if somebody's trigger finger had twitched that night? So Cosgrove was right to praise the cool professionalism of his men, which certainly avoided a crisis and quite possibly a catastrophe. But they should never have been placed in such a position to begin with. That is not to say that they shouldn't have been sent to East Timor, rather that their presence and the grossly magnified consequences of any miscalculation on their part evidenced the collapse of the dysfunctional paradigm embraced by successive Australian governments for managing the relationship with our northern neighbour.

Australian policy, which once encompassed the likelihood of armed conflict with Indonesia as a leading principle, has long sought to avoid such a disaster. This is entirely commendable. Without a commitment to large-scale immigration, Australia's relative strategic standing can only decline over the next century. Consequently, to adopt an adversarial posture towards Indonesia – or whichever state succeeds it, should the republic fragment in the next decade – would constitute the most inept and negligent of stratagems. Consider just some of the relevant geopolitical factors – the increasingly violent atomisation of Melanesia and Polynesia, the institutional decay of Papua New Guinea, the inevitable implosion of North Korea, nuclear competition on the subcontinent, the manifold uncertainties of communist China's future, and the decreasing importance of New Zealand as an economic and military partner. There are precious few reasons for optimism. Even putting aside geopolitical threats, the unavoidable marginalisation of Australia's tiny economy will erode what little leverage it can apply to international affairs at the moment. To be forced to manage all of these challenges while maintaining a bilateral cold war against Indonesia or its successor states would be beyond our capacities.

Herein lies the motivation of a generation of Australian diplomats, soldiers and politicians who struggled, vainly as it turned out, to put aside elemental national differences in the attempt to forge a mature and practical concord between two mismatched nation states. No dishonour attaches to them for making the attempt, but the model adopted, which can be characterised by its wilful blindness towards permanent flaws in Suharto's New Order regime, was of questionable value. Indeed, many questioned our approach to East Timor when it arose as an issue. But it is only now, with that newborn nation in ruins and ties to Jakarta ripped asunder, that the costs of our misjudgment can be quantified. Of course, the prime responsibility for the carnage in East Timor, not just in '99, but over the preceding two and a half decades, lay with the Suharto government and its schizoidal offspring, the interim administration of Habibie. But Australian governments of all political hues bear responsibility for their actions, which gave succour to tyranny in the belief that diplomatic pragmatism demanded nothing less. That the outcome of this failure was not a heavy reckoning in Australian blood and treasure is a testament to the skill and courage of the ADF – and, it must be emphasised, to the efforts of many Indonesians who were determined to avoid the siren song of xenophobic nationalism.

Despite the longstanding and blatant frustration of political elites in both Canberra and Jakarta that the relationship was held hostage to the fate of a small island nation both would rather have forgotten, the fact remains that a hostage it was, and even now remains. East Timor was the prism through which everything else was viewed. It both distorted and defined the relationship between the two countries, and before turning to the future we are obliged to try and understand this past.

THE AUSTRALIAN DISEASE
ON THE
DECLINE
of
LOVE
AND THE RISE OF
NON-FREEDOM
RICHARD FLANAGAN

SHORT ● BLACKS

Richard Flanagan's perceptive, hilarious, searing exposé of the conformity that afflicts our public life.

Fat City
Karen Hitchcock

SHORT ● BLACKS

In a riveting blend of story and analysis, doctor and writer Karen Hitchcock explores chemistry, psychology and impulse to excess to explain the West's growing obesity epidemic.

THE WAR OF THE WORLDS
NOEL PEARSON

SHORT ● BLACKS

Noel Pearson considers
the most confronting issue
of Australian history:
the question of genocide,
in early Tasmania
and elsewhere.

REGIONS OF THICK-RIBBED ICE
HELEN GARNER

SHORT ● BLACKS

Helen Garner tells the tale
of a journey to Antarctica
aboard the *Professor
Molchanov*, spanning
icebergs, tourism, time,
photography and the many
forms of desolation.

THE BRAVE ONES

EAST TIMOR, 1999

JOHN BIRMINGHAM

John Birmingham's unflinching account of the Indonesian Army's Battalion 745 as it withdrew from East Timor after the 1999 independence vote, leaving a trail of devastation in its wake.

BOOZE TERRITORY

ANNA KRIEN

Anna Krien takes a clear-eyed look at Indigenous binge-drinking, and never fails to see the human dimension of an intractable problem, shining a light on its deep causes.

THE ONE DAY
DAVID MALOUF

SHORT ● BLACKS

David Malouf traces the meaning of Anzac Day and shows how what was once history has now passed into legend, and how we have found in Anzac Day 'a truly national occasion.'

Prosper
A voyage at sea
Simon Leys

SHORT ● BLACKS

Simon Leys' exceptionally beautiful and elegiac essay about a summer spent on the crew of a tuna-fishing boat in Brittany.

CYPHERPUNK REVOLUTIONARY
ON JULIAN ASSANGE
ROBERT MANNE

Robert Manne reveals the making of Julian Assange and shows how he became one of the most influential Australians of our time.

KILLING THE BLACK DOG
LES MURRAY

Les Murray's frank and courageous account of his struggle with depression.

NO FIXED ADDRESS
ROBYN DAVIDSON

SHORT ● BLACKS

Robyn Davidson's fascinating and moving essay about nomads explores why, in times of environmental peril, the nomadic way with nature still offers valuable lessons.

TRADITION, TRUTH & TOMORROW
GALARRWUY YUNUPINGU

SHORT ● BLACKS

Galarrwuy Yunupingu tells of his early life, his dealings with prime minsters, and how he learnt that nothing is ever what it seems.